CONTENTS

Acknowledgements

The author and publishers wish to thank the following who have kindly given permission for the use of copyright material:

Elaine Greene Ltd on behalf of Studs Terkel for an extract from *Hard Times*, Copyright © 1970 by Studs Terkel; David Higham Associates Ltd on behalf of Langston Hughes for 'Ballad of Roosevelt', Hill and Wang; Monthly Review Foundation for extracts from *The Politics of US Labor* by David Milton, Copyright © 1982 by David Milton; Murray Pollinger on behalf of John Costello for extracts from *The Pacific War*, Collins and Pan Books.

The author and publishers wish to acknowledge, with thanks, the following photographic sources:

Associated Press p33 bottom; BBC Hulton Picture Library/Bettmann Archive pp10, 16 bottom, 23, 28, 29, 33 top, 33 centre, 45; Library of Congress, USA pp6 right, 31; Peter Newark's Western Americana pp5, 6 left, 16 top, 34, 48, 51, 52, 53, 55; Popperfoto pp8, 14; *Richmond Times Dispatch* p38; Tennessee Valley Authority p21; John Topham Photograph Library pp12, 17; US Navy/MARS, Lincs, England pp44, 47; Wide World Photos p24.

The publishers have made every effort to trace the copyright holders, but if they have inadvertently overlooked any, they will be pleased to make the necessary arrangements at the first opportunity.

PREFACE

The study of history is exciting, whether in a good story well told, a mystery solved by the judicious unravelling of clues, or a study of the men, women and children whose fears and ambitions, successes and tragedies make up the collective memory of mankind.

This series aims to reveal this excitement to pupils through a set of topic books on important historical subjects from the Middle Ages to the present day. Each book contains four main elements: a narrative and descriptive text, lively and relevant illustrations, extracts of contemporary evidence, and questions for further thought and work. Involvement in these elements should provide an adventure which will bring the past to life in the imagination of the pupil.

Each book is also designed to develop the knowledge, skills and concepts so essential to a pupil's growth. It provides a wide, varying introduction to the evidence available on each topic. In handling this evidence, pupils will increase their understanding of basic historical concepts such as causation and change, as well as of more advanced ideas such as revolution and democracy. In addition, their use of basic study skills will be complemented by more sophisticated historical skills such as the detection of bias and the formulation of opinion.

The intended audience for the series is pupils of eleven to sixteen years: it is expected that the earlier topics will be introduced in the first three years of secondary school, while the nineteenth and twentieth century topics are directed towards first examinations.

1 THE FIRST NEW DEAL: 1933

The American Dream

Jack Dempsey, the Manassa Mauler

On 23 September 1926, 120 000 people packed into a rain-swept stadium in Philadelphia to see the most eagerly awaited boxing match of the century. World champion Jack Dempsey, 'The Manassa Mauler', was defending his title against Gene Tunney, 'The Fighting Marine'. Interest in the fight was so great that a further 70 000 people went to the stadium without tickets and with no chance of admission. Millions of others gathered round their wireless sets to hear the fight broadcast through the new miracle of radio.

The ninth of 13 children, Dempsey grew up amid poverty and violence in Manassa, Colorado. His boxing style was savage. One sports writer declared that Dempsey was 'as hard and violent as any man living'. The scowl on Dempsey's unshaven face was said to be enough to terrify many opponents.

The contrast between Dempsey and 'The Fighting Marine' could hardly have been greater. Handsome, tall, blond and unscarred, Gene Tunney represented the values of hard work, clean living and patriotism. Yet the two fighters had something in common. Neither came from a wealthy background, but they had both made a fortune through a combination of talent and hard work. In the prosperous times of the mid-1920s, this was the American Dream.

Tunney's battle for survival against Dempsey's ferocious attacks was watched by an array of stars. Baseball hero Babe Ruth, film star Charlie Chaplin, and millionaire businessman Percy Rockefeller were all at the ringside. Like Dempsey and Tunney, they too represented the American Dream.

That night in Philadelphia the stars rubbed shoulders with thousands of middle-class Americans who had more modest dreams and ambitions. The shorter working hours and higher rates of pay obtained by the middle classes in the 1920s made them eager for entertainment. The boxing was also watched by a large number of women. This would have been unheard of a few years earlier.

Typically, this new generation of Americans spent their money at the cinema and at baseball and football matches. They equipped their homes with washing machines, refrigerators and vacuum cleaners, which they often paid for in monthly instalments. By 1928 the majority of people in this affluent society supported the Republican Party, led by Herbert Hoover.

It is important, however, to note that a large number of Americans did not share in the prosperity of the 1920s. While company profits

Right: *the height of prosperity*

Below: *the depths of poverty. Scene in a railroad yard, Sacramento, California*

soared by an average of 62 per cent during the 1920s, wages rose by an average of only seven per cent. The top five per cent of the country owned 26 per cent of the nation's wealth, while over 60 per cent lived just above the poverty line.

'The Fight of the Century' lived up to its name. Using his brilliant defensive skills, Gene Tunney kept the Manassa Mauler at bay for ten gruelling rounds and was awarded the fight on a points decision. The contest was seen by Americans of all classes. Three years later Americans from every walk of life were affected by a crisis which devastated the USA. The Wall Street Crash of 1929 left the American Dream in tatters.

1932: a bleak winter

America braced itself for the winter of 1932 in the grip of the worst depression in its history. The optimism and prosperity of the 1920s had disappeared. Almost 13 million people were unemployed. More than one million Americans wandered the country in a desperate search for work. Since the start of the Depression in 1929, five thousand banks had gone out of business and nine million people had lost all their savings.

Those who had gambled on the stock market had also met with disaster. So many shares were in circulation by 1929 that inevitably their value declined. On a single day in October 1929, 12 894 650 shares were sold, many of them at prices far below the amount which had originally been paid for them. Between 1929 and 1932, America's industrial production was cut by more than half. The average weekly wage in manufacturing dropped from $24.16 in 1929, to $16.65 in 1933.

One writer recalled that the winter of 1932–3 seemed like the end of the world. He wrote: 'We could smell the depression in the air, it was like a raw wind.' In December 1932, a university professor noted in his diary, 'No one can live and work in New York this winter without a profound sense of uneasiness. Never in modern times has there been so [much] widespread unemployment and such moving distress from sheer hunger and cold.' In Chicago, 50 people were seen fighting over a barrel of garbage behind a restaurant. A shopkeeper in Philadelphia kept one family alive on credit. He described the situation: 'Eleven children in that house. They've got no shoes, no pants. In the house, no chairs. My God, you go in there, you cry, that is all.'

In 1940, Frederick Allen, an American writer, recalled some of the worst features of the Depression:

First, the bread lines in the poorer districts. Second, those bleak settlements ironically known as 'Hoovervilles' in the outskirts of the city and on vacant lots – groups of makeshift shacks constructed out of packing boxes, scrap iron, anything that could be picked up free in a diligent combing of the city dumps. . . . Third, the homeless people sleeping in the doorways or on park benches, and going the rounds of the restaurants for leftover half-eaten biscuits, pie crusts, anything. . . . Fourth, the vastly increased numbers of thumbers on the highway, and particularly of freight-car transients on the railroads; a huge array of drifters ever on the move, searching half-aimlessly for a place where there might be a job.

F.L. Allen: *Since Yesterday*, 1940

Questions

1 Why do you think the settlements described in this source were known as 'Hoovervilles'?

2 The above account was written several years after the events had taken place. In what ways would an account written in 1932 be (a) more reliable, and (b) less reliable?

Hooverville, Los Angeles, 1932

The 1932 election

The American people were bewildered. They did not understand what had gone wrong. The Republican government, led by Herbert Hoover, had claimed credit for the boom of the 1920s as the 'party of prosperity'. Now many people blamed them for the Crash.

Hoover had promised the American people 'a chicken in every pot' and 'a car in every garage'. He urged each person to help themselves and to rely less on the government – he believed in a policy of 'rugged individualism'. In August 1928 he had declared: 'We in America today are nearer to the final triumph over poverty than ever before in the history of any land.' However, four years later the 'final triumph' seemed far away.

In the presidential election of 1932, the American people had a clear choice. They could either give Herbert Hoover and the Republican Party another chance, or they could vote for the Democratic Party, led by the former Governor of New York, Franklin Delano Roosevelt.

Not everyone was convinced that Roosevelt could do any better than Hoover. Roosevelt himself had no personal experience of poverty. His wealthy parents sent him to Groton School and then to Harvard University, two of America's most exclusive educational establishments. In 1921, at the age of 39, Roosevelt was struck down by polio. He would never walk unaided again. In 1932 many people doubted if he had the stamina to stand up to the physically demanding election campaign, let alone the enormous strain of being president. Finally, many of Roosevelt's speeches in the election campaign seemed extremely vague and contradictory. For example, he criticised Hoover's government for spending too much money but promised a massive increase in funds for the unemployed.

Yet Roosevelt had one major asset: most people associated the Crash with Herbert Hoover. Roosevelt did not waste this advantage.

Using the evidence: the 1932 election

A *Hoover is my shepherd, I am in want,*
   He maketh me to lie down on park benches
   He leadeth me by still factories,
   He restoreth my doubt in the Republican Party,
   He guided me in the path of the
   Unemployed for his party's sake.

   E.J. Sullivan: *The 1932nd Psalm*, 1932

B (i) *I pledge you, I pledge myself, to a new deal for the*
        American people.

        F.D. Roosevelt, Chicago, July 1932

   (ii) *I accuse the present Administration of being the greatest*
        spending Administration in peace times in all our history.
        It is an Administration that has failed to anticipate the
        dire needs and the reduced earning power of the
        people.

        F.D. Roosevelt, Iowa, September 1932

   (iii) *I regard reduction in Federal spending as one of the*
         most important issues of this campaign.

         F.D. Roosevelt, Pittsburgh, October 1932

C A cartoon published in
   the *Rochester Chronicle*,
   May 1933

9

Roosevelt (in centre) on the campaign trail

D *This campaign is more than a contest between two men. . . .*
   They are proposing changes and so-called new deals which
   would destroy the very foundations of our American system.
      Our system is founded on the conception that only
   through freedom to the individual will his initiative and
   enterprise be summoned to spur the march of progress.

   Herbert Hoover, New York, October 1932

E *His legs actually became something of a political asset. They*
   won him sympathy, something he might never have had
   otherwise. Millions of Americans were electrified in later
   years by Roosevelt's public appearances – the tense,
   painfully awkward approach to the center of the stage
   climaxed with Roosevelt's radiant smiles and vigorous
   gestures.

   James MacGregor Burns: *Roosevelt,*
   the Lion and the Fox, 1956

F *The president [Hoover], white-faced, exhausted, stumbling in speech, repeatedly losing his place in his manuscript, swayed on the platform. Behind him a man gripped an empty chair to be shoved under him in case of collapse. Colonel Starling, chief of the Secret Service, broke into a cold sweat. After the speech a prominent Republican took Starling aside and said, 'Why don't they make him quit? He's not doing himself or the party any good. It's turning into a farce. He is tired physically and mentally.'*

A.J. Schlesinger: *The Crisis of the Old Order, 1919–1933*, 1957

1 What evidence can you find in these sources to support the idea that Hoover was being blamed for the Crash?

2 Some people felt that Roosevelt's promises were unreliable and vague. Which pieces of evidence support this opinion?

3 Is there enough evidence here to say that Roosevelt stood up to the physical demands of the campaign more successfully than Hoover?

The Wall Street Crash destroyed the Republican Party's chances of victory in the 1932 election. Towards the end of the campaign Hoover seemed a weary man. Historian William Leuchtenburg describes how Hoover was 'often jeered by crowds as a President had never been jeered before'. On election day, 8 November 1932, Roosevelt swept to victory with 22 800 000 votes to Hoover's 15 750 000.

The Crash had brought Roosevelt the presidency, yet he had little time for celebration. Between the election victory and his inauguration in March 1933 Roosevelt had to decide on all the details of his 'new deal'.

The hundred days

On Saturday 4 March 1933, a massive crowd gathered at the Capitol Hill in Washington to hear Roosevelt's first speech as President. The President's expression was grim. His voice rang out as the crowd listened in silence:

First of all, let me assert my firm belief that the only thing we have to fear is fear itself – nameless, unreasoning, unjustified terror.

Roosevelt blamed the country's bankers who, having 'failed through their own stubbornness and their own incompetence, have admitted their failure and have abdicated'. Finally, Roosevelt promised 'action, and action now'.

Franklin D. Roosevelt's inaugural speech, March 1933

The first hundred days of Roosevelt's presidency were hectic and dramatic. The most immediate problem was the banking crisis. As one writer put it, 'Hoover left office to the sound of crashing banks'. Many investors had shown their lack of confidence in the Republican administration by taking their savings out of the banks in suitcases. On the day of Roosevelt's inaugural speech, 38 states had closed their banks.

Roosevelt's response came on 5 March 1933. He declared that the banks should close for several days. It was a brilliant move. It gave people time to regain their nerve. Did they really need to take out all of their savings? When Roosevelt announced government help for private banks, confidence flooded back. The banking crisis was over.

This brilliant success was quickly followed by another. On Sunday 12 March, Roosevelt broadcast the first of his 'fireside chats' to the American people. Sixty million people gathered round their radio sets to hear the President's reassuring words. He told the nation that it was now safe to return their savings to the banks.

A wave of adulation for Roosevelt swept the country. In the week following his inauguration 450 000 letters, nearly all of them favourable, poured into the White House.

Yet there was still much to be done. Almost 13 million people were unemployed. Over the next few months, Roosevelt set up a series of Government agencies with one aim in mind – to get Americans back to work.

The first New Deal	
Agency	*Details*
Tennessee Valley Authority (TVA)	One of the most ambitious New Deal agencies. It was responsible for flood control, building dams and reservoirs, preventing soil erosion and building new towns.
Civil Works Administration (CWA)	At its peak, this agency employed more than four million people, building roads, schools, airports and other public amenities.
Public Works Administration (PWA)	Built hospitals, libraries, town halls and schools.
National Recovery Administration (NRA)	Tried to negotiate agreements with all of the major industries to produce fair prices, wages and working hours. More than two million employers displayed a Blue Eagle symbol to show they were taking part in the scheme.

THE RURAL DEPRESSION

Years of poverty

For most American farmers the 1920s were years of poverty and hardship. The prosperity enjoyed in the towns did not extend to the countryside. The basic problem was overproduction. When America entered World War I in 1917, the government encouraged farmers to produce as much cotton and wheat as possible, and to raise the maximum number of cattle and sheep. When the war ended in 1918, America's farmers continued to produce as much as they could. Eventually they were producing more wheat and cotton than they could possibly sell. This meant that farm produce was selling at prices far below the cost of production. Investigators discovered that some farmers were earning as little as $89 a year.

This song, written by Bob Miller in the 1930s, describes how the problem of overproduction affected farmers:

Seven cent cotton and forty cent meat,
How in the world can a poor man eat?
Poor getting poorer all around here,
Kids coming regular every year.
Fatten our hogs, take 'em to town,
All we get is six cents a pound.
Very next day we have to buy it back.
Forty cents a pound in a paper sack.

Many victims of the dust bowl endured terrible conditions

Such low incomes meant severe poverty. The majority of farmers lived in small shacks with tin roofs, no electricity, no running water and, in many cases, no toilets. Diseases caused by a combination of malnutrition and unhygienic living conditions were rife.

The horrors of the dust bowl

For many farmers the hardship of the 1920s must have seemed minor compared to the nightmare which followed. In 1932 there was no rain in the farming states of Arkansas, Oklahoma, Nebraska, North Dakota and South Dakota. It did not rain again for four years. In 1934 the temperature in Vinita, Oklahoma, topped 100°F for 35 consecutive days; on the thirty-sixth day the heat reached a searing 117°F. Farmers could only stand and watch as cattle dropped dead in their tracks. Across the whole region scorched top soil became as dry as dust. The intense heat was followed by fierce winds which blew the dry top soil away. Farming land which until 1932 had been green and fertile now took on the appearance of a desert. America's main farming region had been reduced to a dust bowl.

When the rains returned they brought further disaster. On one small lowland farm in Akron, Colorado, it rained for the first time in two years in June 1934. A massive electrical storm brought an immense downpour. The farmer's joy at the sight of rain soon turned to terror. The dry top soil was swept away in a raging torrent. His barns and home were soon under water. He managed to drag his wife and screaming children to a small hillock from where they were later rescued by the fire department. The farmer and his family had survived but his livelihood had been destroyed.

During the 1930s millions of American farmers and their families went through similar experiences. Unlike the farmer from Akron, however, many did not survive.

Using the evidence: the dust bowl

A   *Between 1934 and 1938 prolonged drought dried up millions of acres of farmland and pasturage between the Appalachians and the Rockies and dust storms of unprecedented violence darkened the skies from Texas to New York. Floods, hurricanes and tornadoes spread havoc throughout the Middle West.*

Floods and windstorms during that period took 3,678 lives, injured 18,791 and destroyed or damaged 559,164 buildings.

R. Cabell-Philips: *From the Crash to the Blitz*, 1969

B Aftermath of the drought: a dead Longhorn in Sioux County, Nebraska.

C *I proceeded to tell that gentleman about the children I'd seen running about with bare feet in Bottineau County, North Dakota, in zero weather last autumn, about the farmers in South Dakota who were clawing up mildewed Russian thistle out of the stacks they had cut for their cattle and making it into soup.... About cattle I'd seen so weak they could hardly walk....*

Lorena Hickok, *One Third of a Nation*, 1981

D *We got in the car and drove through the sizzling countryside. We stop and talk to a farmer. His eyes are bloodshot. I can hardly see from the heat and terrible emotion.... We both know that the farmer across the river shot twenty-two of his cattle yesterday, and then shot himself.*

W. Stott: *Documentary Expression and Thirties America*, 1973

E After a dust storm: buried machinery on a farm, 1936.

F *It was during the grasshopper days in 1933. The sun was shining brightly when we left home. When we were about halfway it just turned dark. It was the grasshoppers that covered the sun. Our neighbours said: 'The grasshoppers have come in, they've taken every leaf off our trees, they're even starting to eat the fence posts.' I thought that was a joke.*

Quoted in Studs Terkel's book, *Hard Times*, 1970

1   What signs of rural poverty are contained in these sources?

2   Why were the farmers described in the sources unable to keep their cattle alive?

3   In *Hard Times*, published in 1970, the writer Studs Terkel asked people to recall their memories of the 1930s. Extract **F** is one such memory. How reliable is this piece of evidence?

4   Compare the photographs with the written accounts. Which type of evidence do you think is most effective in showing the real impact of the Rural Depression?

Hard travelling

During the 1930s approximately one million Americans made what was for many the most dangerous journey of their lives. The farmers of Arkansas and Oklahoma had seen their land turned to dust.

Traveller on the road. South Dakota, 1936

Desperate for work and faced with starvation, they headed for California. The journey to the 'Golden West' was long, difficult and sometimes terrifying.

Using the evidence: the journey west

A *Highway 66 is the main migrant road. 66 – the long concrete path across the country . . . twisting into the mountains . . . down into the bright and terrible desert, and across the desert to the mountains again, and into the rich California valleys. . . .*

The people in flight streamed out on 66, sometimes a single car, sometimes a little caravan. . . . In the day ancient leaky radiators sent up columns of steam, loose connecting rods hammered and pounded. And the men driving the trucks and the overloaded cars listened apprehensively. How far between towns? It is a terror between towns. If something breaks . . . how much food we got? . . . Maybe a bearing's startin' to go. Jesus, if it's a bearing, what'll we do? Money's goin' fast. . . . 'F we can on'y get to California where the oranges grow before this here ol' jub blows up. 'F we on'y can.

ol' jub: old car

John Steinbeck: *The Grapes of Wrath*, 1939

B Members of a Missouri family stranded near Tracy, California. They described their situation as 'broke, baby sick, car trouble'.

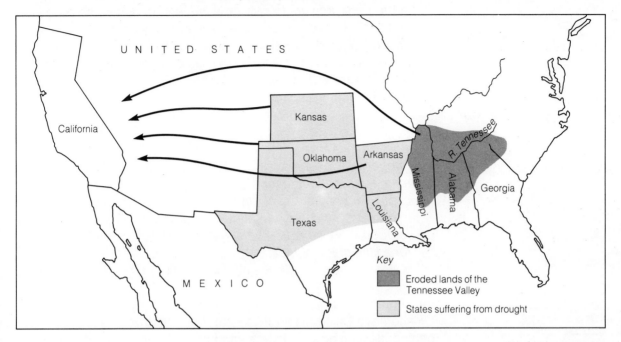

1 What motives did the farmers of Arkansas and Oklahoma have for their journey?

2 Source **A** comes from a novel written in the 1930s. What are (a) the advantages and (b) the disadvantages of such a source?

Journey's end

For those who survived the horrendous journey west the cruellest part was yet to come. Many migrants were turned away at the state border by the Californian police. For those who did get through there was only disappointment. The people of California viewed the 'Okies' and the 'Arkies' with hostility and contempt. The promised land was a land of despair.

Using the evidence: the promised land

A *Tom looking at the ragged peaks across the river said:*
'Never seen such tough mountains. This here's the bones of a country. I seen pitchers of a country flat an' green an' with little houses.... Get to thinkin' they ain't no such country.'
Pa said: 'Wait till we get to California. You'll see nice country then.'
  'Jesus Christ, Pa! This here is California.'
          John Steinbeck: *The Grapes of Wrath*, 1939

B *I believe there is some sort of state law in California compelling growers to provide some sort of decent housing and sanitation for the seasonal workers they employ. . . . These labourers move in with their families, thousands and thousands of them, living in colonies of tents or shacks built of cardboard with no sanitation whatever. There was a good deal of sickness in some camps last winter.*

Lorena Hickok: *One Third of a Nation*, 1981

C *And the migrants streamed in on the highways and their hunger was in their eyes. . . . When there was work for a man, ten men fought for it. . . . If that fella'll work for thirty cents, I'll work for twenty-five. If he'll take twenty-five, I'll do it for twenty. No, me, I'm hungry. I'll work for fifteen. I'll work for food. . . . The kids. You ought to see them. . . . I'll work for a little piece of meat.*

John Steinbeck: *The Grapes of Wrath*, 1939

Imagine that your family have just made the terrifying journey from Oklahoma to California. Write a letter to a friend you have left behind, describing your journey and the difficulties you and your fellow travellers experienced. Tell your friend about the attitude of Californians towards Okies and say whether the 'Golden West' has lived up to expectations.

Finish your letter with practical advice to your friend who may decide to make the same journey.

Roosevelt and the farmers

Not all farmers abandoned their land. Those who stayed behind looked to Roosevelt for help.

Using the evidence: a new deal for farmers

The year is 1933. Emergency measures are needed to save America's farmers. You are an adviser to Roosevelt's Secretary for Agriculture, Henry Wallace. First compile a list of three major problems facing the farmers, and then suggest some possible solutions.

Now compare your findings with what Roosevelt actually did for the farmers. The following sources give examples of the work of three key agencies: the Tennessee Valley Authority, the Civilian Conservation Corps and the Agricultural Adjustment Agency.

A Before 1933 both sides of this hill were eroded. The owner of the farm on the left then took part in a test demonstration scheme for the Tennessee Valley Authority.

B *Indispensible to the work of soil conservation and reforestation was the Civilian Conservation Corps. By September 1935, over 500,000 young men lived in C.C.C. camps. They thinned four million acres of trees, built more than 30,000 wildlife shelters, restored Revolutionary and Civil War battlefields.*
William Leuchtenburg: *F.D.R. and the New Deal*, 1963

The Agricultural Adjustment Agency tried to raise prices for farming produce by destroying surplus crops and livestock. It seemed ironic that while some people starved, this New Deal agency was paying compensation to farmers who agreed to their food reserves being destroyed.

C *Wallace reluctantly agreed (on behalf of the Agricultural Adjustment Agency) to a proposal by farm leaders to forestall a glut in the hog market by slaughtering over six million little pigs and more than two hundred thousand cows which were due to farrow . . . the piglets overran the stock-yards and scampered through the streets of Chicago . . . the country was horrified.*
William Leuchtenburg: *F.D.R. and the New Deal*, 1963

1 Look carefully at the photograph. What steps have been taken by the farmer on the left to combat soil erosion? Source B may help you to answer this question.

2 Suggest two reasons why many people were very angry about the slaughter of the pigs, as described in source C.

3 | A NEW DEAL FOR BLACK PEOPLE?

The Scottsboro boys

It was 1.30 p.m. on Wednesday 25 March 1931. At the Stevenson Railroad Station, in Alabama, the station master looked up from his desk to see a small group of white youths, one of whom was bleeding heavily from a head wound. The boys claimed that 'a bunch of niggers' had thrown them from the Chattanooga to Memphis freight train, which had passed through Stevenson 30 minutes earlier. The white boys wanted to 'press charges' against the blacks.

The station master telephoned Scottsboro, the next town down the line, and was told that the train had passed through minutes before. The next stop was Paint Rock, 68 kilometres from Stevenson.

The matter now came into the hands of Jackson County Sheriff, M.L. Wann. He telephoned his deputy at Paint Rock, Charlie Latham. His instructions to Latham were clear: 'Get to the station. Capture every Negro on the train and bring them back to Scottsboro. Deputise every man you can find.'

Just before two o'clock the train came into sight and before it stopped moving Charlie Latham and his newly recruited posse were on board. They found nine black boys and two young white girls dressed in overalls.

At first, Latham was too busy rounding up the blacks to be concerned about the white girls. It took 20 minutes for Latham and his men to tie the blacks together with a piece of rope and load them into the back of an open truck. The two white girls, Ruby Bates and Victoria Price, now told Latham that they had been raped by all nine black boys. They repeated the allegation when they arrived with the black boys in Scottsboro. No effort was made to keep the charges

The route of the train on which the alleged rape took place

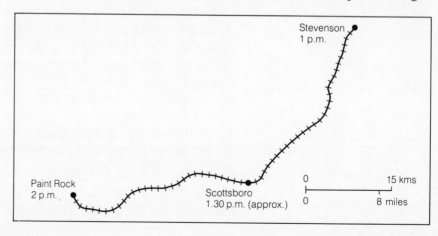

22

The Scottsboro boys under armed guard

confidential and by late afternoon townspeople told how the 'black brutes had chewed off one of the breasts of Ruby Bates'. Before long, the crowd outside Scottsboro jail had become a mob and a lynching was in the air.

At 8.30 p.m. Sheriff Wann decided that the angry mob was going to rush the jail at any moment. Twenty-five armed men were needed to get the boys to a sturdier lock-up. Sheriff Wann had saved the boys from a lynching and the stage was set for the case to become the most sensational trial of the 1930s.

Jackson County's two weekly newspapers did not doubt that the blacks were guilty. The *Scottsboro Progressive Age* exclaimed that 'the details of the crime coming from the lips of the two girls are too revolting to be printed. They are being treated for injuries sustained when assaulted by these Negroes'. The *Jackson County Sentinel* declared, 'All Negroes positively identified. Girls held prisoner with pistol and knives while nine black fiends committed revolting crimes'.

Questions

1 What definite facts are contained in the story so far?

2 Which aspects mentioned so far do you regard as unreliable?

3 Many local people seemed quick to accept as fact the rumours of what the boys had done. What do you think was the reason for this?

23

Before the trial, William Patterson, a leading member of a Communist organisation called the International Labour Defence, took up the cause of the nine black boys who had now become known as the 'Scottsboro boys'. In 1970 he talked about the events that followed. This type of evidence is called oral history.

> *I immediately sought the services of Samuel Liebovitz. He was one of New York's leading criminal lawyers and he had never lost a death case.... Liebovitz handled the case in a masterly fashion. The freight train on which these lads were riding had forty-nine cars. Liebovitz had a replica made of this train with every car placed in the position it originally occupied. In the trial, he forced the complainants, these two white girls, to show what car the rape had taken place in. He showed the judge that this car had been full of gravel, that the gravel had come up to the level of the car's sides. Had these girls been raped, their backs would have been lacerated....*
>
> Quoted in Studs Terkel's book, *Hard Times*, 1970

Liebovitz's defence of the boys was strengthened still further when, in January 1932, Ruby Bates confessed to a friend that no rape had taken place:

> *She told how she had been threatened with imprisonment unless she charged these boys with rape. She told how Victoria Price, the other girl, had been implicated in a murder charge, and how this threat of prosecution was held over her head.... Ruby found it impossible to be party to a crime of this magnitude.*
>
> Quoted in Studs Terkel's book, *Hard Times*, 1970

Despite Ruby Bates' evidence, five of the nine boys were still in prison in 1938, serving 75-year sentences. President Roosevelt was

The jury at the boys' trial. Can you draw any conclusions from this photograph about the fairness of the trial?

told that the prosecution's case was based on 'a mass of contradictions and improbabilities'. On 7 December 1938, Roosevelt sent a letter to the Governor of Alabama, Bibb Graves.

> *Dear Bibb,*
>
> *I am sorry indeed not to have seen you while I was at Warm Springs because I wanted to give you a purely personal, and not in any way official, suggestion. You have been such a grand Governor that I want you to go out of office without the loss of the many friends that you have made throughout the nation. There was a real feeling in very wide circles that you said definitely and positively that you were going to commute the sentences of the remainder of the Scottsboro boys. . . . The boys could be taken away from Alabama with a guarantee on their part that they would not turn up again.*
>
> *As I said before, I am writing this only as a very old and warm friend of yours, and I hope you will take it in the spirit it is said.*

When the request was refused the President decided to remain silent. By 1940, the story had disappeared from the headlines but the five men – they were no longer boys – were still in prison. On 9 June 1950, the last of the Scottsboro boys was finally released. Andrew Wright was granted parole, 19 years and two months after he had been taken from the train at Paint Rock, Alabama. 'I have no hard feelings,' Wright told reporters. 'I'm not mad because Mrs Price lied about me. If she's still living, I feel sorry for her because I guess she don't sleep much at night.'

Using the evidence

You are on the platform at Paint Rock station just before the Scottsboro boys are arrested. Write an account, based on what you have read, of each of the following:
a)   the opinions of the white people around you;
b)   the atmosphere shortly before and just after the boys are arrested;
c)   the rumours which develop.

Lynching

Many blacks were treated even more harshly than the Scottsboro boys:

> *From 1933 to 1935, lynch mobs murdered sixty-three Negroes while southern sheriffs often looked the other way. In 1937, a mob in Duck Hill, Mississippi, took two Negroes from a jail, set them on fire with blowtorches, then ghoulishly hanged them.*
>
>   R. Polenberg: *One Nation Divisible*, 1980

*On October 19, 1934, a young Negro, Claude Neal, was arrested
for murder in Marianna, Florida. To avoid the angry public mood,
officials moved Neal from jail to jail. On Friday, October 26,
however, he was seized by mob action at Brewton, Alabama, and
transported back to Marianna where a crowd of over four thousand
awaited a lynching. Subjected to the most brutal treatment, Neal
was finally hanged by the neck in the court house square. Local
police failed to maintain order....*

B. Sternsher: *The Negro in Depression and War*, 1969

Civil rights campaigners responded to the increase in violence against
blacks by drawing up an anti-lynching bill. Northern Democrats
expressed support for the bill, but Roosevelt was not prepared to risk
losing the support of southern whites by helping the blacks. In May
1934 he told a black rights spokesman:

*I've got to get legislation passed by Congress to save America. The
Southerners occupy strategic places on most of the Senate and House
committees. If I come out for the anti-lynching bill now, they will
block every bill I ask Congress to pass to keep America from
collapsing.*

Without the President's help, the anti-lynching bill came to nothing.
The painful truth is that not a single civil rights measure was
adopted in Roosevelt's four terms in the White House.

Questions

1 a) From the accounts of the lynchings, pick out the phrases
      which give information on:
       i) location
      ii) public opinion
     iii) attitude of the law
      iv) treatment of blacks.
   b) What conclusions do you draw from this information?

2 Look again at F.D.R.'s comments of May 1934 and his letter to
   Bibb Graves, written in 1938. Describe how Roosevelt's public
   attitude to black rights differed from his private attitude.

Poverty

*The Negro was born in depression. It didn't mean much to him. The
Great Depression as you call it. There was no such thing. The best
he could be is a janitor or porter or a shoeshine boy. It only became
official when it hit the white man.*

Clifford Burke, quoted in Studs Terkel's book,
Hard Times, 1970

It was only after the Crash in 1929 and the onset of mass unemployment among whites, that the government began to take action to relieve poverty.

According to official government estimates, unemployment rose from 1.6 million in 1929 to 12.8 million in 1933. So for many ordinary white Americans the Crash was a vivid and dramatic turning point between prosperity and poverty. However, the majority of blacks who made up one tenth of America's population had never known anything other than poverty. This poverty was most severe for the three million blacks who farmed in the south.

> *Typically, they lived in two to three room unpainted cabins, without screens, doors, plumbing, electricity, running water or sanitary wells. Most tenants had not received any cash income in years. Disease was rampant; there were two million cases of Malaria alone in 1938.*
>
> J. Patterson: *America's Struggle Against Poverty*, 1981

When the Crash came, the blacks had one advantage, according to Clifford Burke:

> *Our wives, they could go to the store and get a bag of beans or a sack of flour and piece of fat meat, and they could cook this. And we could eat it.... Now you take the white fella, he couldn't do this.... He couldn't stand bringing home beans instead of steak or capon. And he couldn't stand the idea of going on relief like a Negro.*
>
> Clifford Burke, quoted in Studs Terkel's book,
> *Hard Times*, 1970

Employment

According to the 1940 census, only one in 20 black males was employed in a white-collar occupation, compared to one in three white males. Twice as many blacks as whites farmed, but a much smaller proportion worked their own land. Among white women who worked, one in ten was employed as a maid; among black women, six out of ten were similarly employed.

The Depression made things worse for blacks mainly because, as unemployment soared, many whites resorted to the menial jobs which had previously been regarded as fit only for blacks. Lorena Hickock, one of Roosevelt's official researchers, was told by an unemployed white woman, 'I'd do anything if only I could get a job, even nigger work.'

In the Deep South, where more than three-quarters of America's black population lived, blacks were almost completely excluded from responsible jobs. In 1940, there was not a single black policeman in the states of Mississippi, South Carolina, Louisiana, Georgia and Alabama.

27

Working as a shoe-shine boy was a typical black occupation. How would racial prejudice be reinforced through this type of work?

Segregation

We go into a café (in L.A.) 'cause there was no train out 'till eleven that night. In comes a Mexican whore and a colored whore. They order a hamburger. The proprietor says, 'I don't serve niggers. Get that dame out of here.' [They leave.] The Mexican girl comes back and orders two hamburgers. The guy grumbles, fires up a couple. The colored girl walks in. This guy goes under the counter and comes up with a sap. He lashes out at the girl's head, bong! I think he's killed her. He cuts around the corner in a wild rage. I put out my foot and trip him. The girls get out in time. He'd a killed that girl, I believe.

sap: a leather-covered club with a weighted head

Ed Paulsen, quoted in Studs Terkel's book, *Hard Times*, 1970

In the Deep South, and in many other areas, blacks had to use separate waiting rooms at stations, attend their own schools and churches and eat at separate restaurants.

Blacks were constantly reminded of their inferior status. For example, no matter how old they were, blacks were inevitably referred to by southern whites as 'boy' or 'girl'; and until the 1940s the American Red Cross kept black people's blood segregated in blood banks.

Segregation in the 1930s.
Above: *at a cinema.*
Right: *at a drinking fountain*

Question

Look carefully at the photographs on this page, then write a paragraph or two on how you think black people must have felt about segregation.

The black vote

The vast majority of southern blacks did not vote in the presidential election of 1932. Voters had to pay a poll tax of about $2, and few blacks could afford this. Even if they could afford to pay the tax, fear of violence and intimidation at the polling stations normally prevented them from voting.

Elsewhere, the Democratic Party struggled to gain black support. In the 1932 election, Roosevelt won 59 per cent of the white vote in Chicago, but only 23 per cent of the black vote. Urban centres such as Detroit, Cleveland and Philadelphia had a large black electorate, but in 1932 they mainly supported Hoover. At first, it seemed unlikely that the early New Deal agencies would be able to change this situation.

Some of the early New Deal projects provoked hostility from black leaders, often justifiably. The pride of the Tennessee Valley Authority was its new model town of Norris. This 'vision of villages and clean small factories' contained new houses, farm buildings and dams. However, black people were outraged to find that only white people would be allowed to live there. Even in one of the great showplaces of the New Deal, blacks still found themselves being discriminated against.

Some other New Deal agencies seemed equally unhelpful. The Civilian Conservation Corps, which employed young men on the nation's farms, forests and parks, usually had segregated camps for the workers. The reaction of the citizens of Thornhurst, Pennsylvania, to rumours of all-black camps being set up in their neighbourhood, was fairly typical:

> *Many unescorted women of various ages are obliged to travel by the site of these camps at all hours of the day or night.... They should not be exposed to possible, indeed probable, dangers.*
>
> Extract from a petition dated 30 October 1934

In 1935, the black newspaper *Crisis* told its readers that they 'ought to realise by now that the powers-that-be in the Roosevelt administration have nothing for them'.

But, surprisingly, by 1936 blacks had clearly begun to move away from the Republican Party. That year, every black constituency in Cleveland voted for the Democrats, and F.D.R.'s black vote in Chicago was twice what it had been in 1932. In 1938, a Chicago magazine poll recorded that 84 per cent of the blacks who were interviewed were pro-Roosevelt.

Why did blacks begin to support Roosevelt? In many areas blacks were hit harder than any other group by the Depression. They survived mainly because of the relief cheques paid out by Roosevelt. The number of blacks on relief increased from about 18 per cent of the black population in October 1933, to almost 30 per cent in January 1935. Blacks began to vote for Roosevelt because they felt that they owed their survival to him.

THE SECOND NEW DEAL: 1934-8

1934 – no men wanted!

In the summer of 1934, Roosevelt toured the United States for the first time since his election victory of 1932. He was pleased with what he saw:

> *They were hopeful people. They had courage written all over their faces. They looked cheerful . . . whereas in 1932 there was a look of despair.*

John Major: *The New Deal*, 1968

No work today. Washington DC

Roosevelt felt that the emergency measures of the first New Deal had succeeded. He had staved off total disaster. The banks remained open. In the letters that flooded into the White House many working-class Americans hailed Roosevelt as their saviour. A woman from Wisconsin wrote, 'We all feel if there ever was a saint, he is one.'

Yet the problem of unemployment still troubled Roosevelt. In his first New Deal (1933), he had spent millions of dollars on various government agencies to try to get unemployment down from the peak of 12.8 million. Despite all these efforts, 11.3 million were still without work at the start of 1934.

A character in a novel written in 1934 exclaimed: 'What the hell has happened to everything? You read in the paper things have never been so good; there's never been so much prosperity; the God-damned stock-market is booming; and then you find out you can't get work; everybody's losing his job, or their wages are being cut.'

Questions

1 The extract from the novel includes a reference to wages being cut. Can you suggest why this was happening during the Depression?

2 The character in the novel is criticising Roosevelt. Is this type of evidence useful to the historian?

Criticisms of Roosevelt were not confined to literature. More and more ordinary people felt that the President had failed to keep the promises he had made in 1933. One unemployed man wrote to the President to complain:

You promised us work. Give it to us now. We waited long enough.
Quoted in R.S. McElvaine's book, *Down and Out in the Great Depression*, 1983

The feeling of optimism that had been created during the 'hundred days' now turned to a mood of anger. A council meeting in Minneapolis in April 1934 was interrupted by a 6 000-strong mob, armed with sticks, stones and bottles. Their demand had a familiar ring. They wanted work.

Opposition to Roosevelt

In 1933 Roosevelt was criticised for the failings of the New Deal, and support was growing for his opponents. Three men in particular attracted enough support to worry the President. They were Charles Coughlin, Francis Townsend and Huey Long.

Father Charles Coughlin

Coughlin was a Canadian priest who had settled in Royal Oak, Detroit. His radio sermons on the CBS network were a phenomenal success. Coughlin put forward plans to nationalise the banks and to introduce a minimum annual wage.

Dr Francis Townsend

Townsend gained much of his support from old people. He proposed to pay a pension of $200 a month to every American over 60. In return, they had to retire at 60 and spend their $200 within the month, in the United States. Townsend argued that retirement at 60 would create more jobs for younger people. The rapid spending of pension money would increase demand for consumer goods and create more jobs.

Above: *Charles Coughlin*

Right: *Texas billboard advertising Townsend's old age pension plan*

Below: *Huey Long surrounded by bodyguards*

Huey Long

No opponent of Roosevelt was more dangerous than 'the Kingfish', Huey Long. Long was the Governor of the state of Louisiana. He was also determined to replace Roosevelt as President of the United States. He gained national popularity with his 'Share Our Wealth' campaign. If elected, he promised to confiscate all personal fortunes over three million dollars, so that every American would receive between $4 000 and $5 000.

Roosevelt knew that his most powerful weapon against his opponents would be to get people back to work and to bring about full economic recovery. However, all hopes of economic recovery were dashed when, in 1934, 1.5 million workers participated in a total of 1 800 strikes. The unions campaigned for better working conditions, shorter working hours and higher pay. The fact that most employers would not even accept the right of their workers to form unions set the scene for the most bitter industrial disputes in American history.

33

Using the evidence: strike!

A The national background

1 a

Union membership (in thousands)		Days lost through strikes (in thousands)	
Year		Year	
1930	3 632	1930	3 320
1932	3 226	1932	10 500
1934	3 249	1934	19 600
1936	4 164	1936	13 900
1938	8 265	1938	9 150

2 *We are half fed because we can't feed ourselves and [our] families with what we make. And we can't go to a cut-rate store and buy food because ... the company forbids such trading.... And the companies keep their food stuffs at high prices at all times.*

Letter from a miner in Harlan County, 8 June 1932

3 *Employees shall have the right to organise and bargain collectively through representatives of their own choosing ... no employee and no one seeking employment shall be required as a condition of employment to join any company union.*

Extract from Clause 7a of the National Industrial Recovery Act, 1933

4 *Rush says the boss,*
Work like a hoss;
I'll take the profits and you take the loss,
I've got the brains, I've got the dough,
The Lord himself decreed it so.

Strike song: 'Mammy's Little Baby Loves a Union Shop', 1930s

5 *Private police of the Ford Motor Company assault a trade unionist for handing out leaflets, May 1937*

34

6   *A check list of all union sympathisers and strike leaders was kept by the chief of police. Strike leaders were automatically arrested and when released were picked up by company thugs, often through pre-arrangement with the police, taken out into the country, and brutally beaten.*
D. Milton: *The Politics of U.S. Labor*, 1982

B   Case study: the strike of the San Francisco longshoremen, 1934

1   *The demands agreed upon were brief and to the point. They asked for an hourly wage of one dollar, a thirty hour week, a six hour day and regulation of all hiring through the union.*
Demands of striking longshoremen,
San Francisco, February 1934

2   *When no agreement had been reached after nearly a month of negotiations, the longshoremen went out on strike in San Francisco, Seattle, Tacoma, Portland . . . and all other Pacific coast ports.*
D. Milton: *The Politics of U.S. Labor*, 1982

3   *Communists are throwing a monkey wrench into the situation. San Francisco ought to be informed of the growth of the Red element in the situation. There is an element among the longshoremen that lives on strikes and does not want a settlement.*
Edward McGrady, Assistant Secretary of Labor, May 1934

4   *The longshoremen are now represented by spokesmen who are not representative of American labor and who do not desire a settlement of their strike, but who desire a complete paralysis of shipping and industry and who are responsible for the violence and bloodshed which is typical of their tribe. . . . There can be no hope for industrial peace until communistic agitators are removed as the official spokesmen of labor and American leaders are·chosen, to settle their differences along American lines.*
J.W. Maillard, Chairman of San Francisco Chamber of
Commerce, May 1934

5   *On the afternoon of July 3 . . . five trucks, loaded with . . . cargo and escorted by eight police cars rolled out of Pier 38. Police Captain Thomas Hoertkorn, standing on the running board of the lead patrol car, waved his revolver in the air and shouted, 'The port is open!'*

*After a tense period of watching the unloading of ...
cargo at a nearby warehouse, thousands of longshoremen
and their allies finally attacked the reinforced police ranks
with bricks. The police responded with gunfire and tear gas.
One strikebreaker was killed, thirteen policemen and twelve
workers seriously wounded.*

D. Milton: *The Politics of U.S. Labor*, 1982

Questions

1 Look carefully through the evidence in section **A**. What motives
for strike action are shown in these sources?

2 Can you suggest why the employers were reluctant to
recognise the unions?

3 In source 3, section **B**, Edward McGrady claims that the
longshoremen were being led by Communists. J.W. Maillard
makes a similar claim in source 4. Why would they make such
claims?

4 Sources 3 and 4 present the longshoremen in an unfavourable
light. Does the other evidence in section **B** support or
contradict this view?

5 Source 5, section **B**, was written in 1982. How does the
usefulness of this source compare with an eye-witness
account?

The second New Deal (1935)

Roosevelt seemed to be under pressure from all directions. Eleven
million people were still without work, and bitter strike action had
devastated key industries. Coughlin, Townsend and Long were at
the peak of their popularity. Roosevelt's Agricultural Adjustment
Act and the National Recovery Administration had been declared
unconstitutional by the Supreme Court. Before the next presidential
election, which was due in 1936, Roosevelt had to do something to
restore his own popularity. All of these factors combined together to
push Roosevelt into introducing a second New Deal, launched in the
summer of 1935.

The first New Deal had concentrated on emergency action to bring
about economic recovery. The second New Deal introduced the largest
welfare programme in American history. The man who had criticised
Hoover's government for spending too much money, now announced
plans to spend a record amount – $4 800 billion – on poor relief. The main
measures of the second New Deal are shown in the following table.

*Federal expenditure
(in billion dollars)*

Year	
1932	4.7
1933	4.6
1934	6.7
1935	6.5
1936	8.5
1937	7.8
1938	6.8
1939	8.9

The second New Deal, 1935

Agency/Act	Details
The Works Progress Administration (WPA)	One third of the money allotted to poor relief went to the Works Progress Administration (WPA). It employed people to construct hospitals, schools and other public buildings.
The Rural Electrification Administration	This agency aimed to bring electricity to America's farms. Before it was set up, nine out of ten American farms had no electricity supply. Under the Rural Electrification scheme groups of farmers joined together to borrow money from the government to build power lines. It was a huge success. By 1941, four out of ten American farmers had electricity. By 1951, the figure had reached nine out of ten.
The National Labor Relations Act (Wagner Act)	This Act was designed to bring peace between workers and employers after the violent disputes of 1934. It gave firm government backing to the right of workers to form unions. Employers were obliged to accept the formation of unions peacefully.

The presidential election of 1936

The measures introduced in the second New Deal marked the beginning of Roosevelt's campaign to be re-elected for a second term. Roosevelt hoped that the massive sums being paid out to the poor and the unemployed would distract attention from the fact that nine million people were still out of work.

Roosevelt was confident of victory. Support for Coughlin and Townsend had dwindled since 1934, and Huey Long, Roosevelt's most dangerous opponent, had been assassinated in 1935. Added to this the Republican candidate, Alfred Landon, was described – by a member of his own party – as a 'pretty poor specimen'.

Despite his optimism, even Roosevelt was surprised by the size of his victory. He polled 27 752 309 votes to Landon's 16 682 524.

The Supreme Court

The Supreme Court is the highest legal authority in the United States. In 1936 it consisted of nine judges. One of the most important tasks of the court was to keep a balance between the power given to the national government in Washington and the power given to each individual state under the Constitution. The Supreme Court could decide whether interference by the national government in the affairs of a particular state was constitutional or not.

Roosevelt regarded the Supreme Court as an old enemy. Several times since 1933 the Court had ruled that New Deal agencies were

acting unconstitutionally. The President felt that the judges were
making it impossible for him to govern the United States; he decided
that the time had come for him to take on the Supreme Court.

On 5 February 1937 Roosevelt announced his proposals for reform
of the Supreme Court. He began by casting doubt on the ability of
'aged or infirm' judges to deal properly with a large volume of
important work. He proposed that if any judge stayed on for any
longer than six months after his seventieth birthday, the President
could compensate by adding a new, younger judge, of his own
choice.

It did not take long for people to realise that what Roosevelt really
wanted was a court which would give decisions in his favour. The
fact that Roosevelt had tried to cover up his real intentions made

both his supporters and his enemies very angry. Some people accused Roosevelt of trying to take too much power into his own hands. A woman from South Carolina wrote to her senator, 'Don't let that wild man in the White House do this dreadful thing to our country.'

Roosevelt's plans were defeated and his public image was badly damaged. The adverse publicity coincided with something even worse. The economy slumped as the country ran into another recession. The days of the New Deal were numbered.

1937: the recession

At the start of 1937 the country seemed well on the way to recovery. In the spring, industrial output finally rose above the levels of 1929. Unemployment was down to 7.7 million, partly because of the jobs created in the second New Deal. The stock market seemed stable. Then in August 1937 everything went wrong and memories of the collapse of 1929 came flooding back. Industrial activity fell away with the most dramatic drop in the country's history. Steel production fell from 80 per cent of capacity to 19 per cent, in the space of three months; seven million shares were sold on the stock market in a single day; new cars remained unsold in the showrooms. Worried that his government was spending too much money, Roosevelt himself took the decision to lay off thousands of workers employed by the Works Progress Administration. During what people called the 'Roosevelt recession' unemployment soared, so that by 1938 over ten million people were once again without work.

William Leuchtenburg, a historian, summed up the central failing of the New Deal: 'It never demonstrated that it could achieve prosperity in peace time. As late as 1941, the unemployed still numbered six million and not until the war year of 1943 did the army of jobless finally disappear.' Ironically, it was the war rather than the New Deal which brought prosperity back to America.

USA unemployment
(as percentage of labour force)

Year	
1929	3.2
1930	8.7
1931	15.9
1932	23.6
1933	24.9
1934	21.7
1935	20.1
1936	16.9
1937	14.3
1938	19.0
1939	11.2
1940	14.6
1941	9.9

5 ROOSEVELT'S FOREIGN POLICY

I have seen war on land and sea. I have seen blood running from the wounded. I have seen men coughing out their gassed lungs. I have seen the dead in the mud. I have seen cities destroyed.... I hate war.

Franklin D. Roosevelt, 14 August 1936

'The good neighbor'

In his long inaugural speech of 4 March 1933, Roosevelt made only one reference to foreign affairs:

In the field of World policy I would dedicate this nation to the policy of the good neighbor – who resolutely respects himself and, because he does so, respects the rights of others.

Roosevelt knew that the American people wanted to see their country put back on its feet. Almost 13 million people were unemployed and they wanted their jobs back. This was far more important to them than foreign affairs.

The 'neighbors' that F.D.R. had in mind were the Latin American countries such as Brazil, Cuba, Chile, Peru and Paraguay. Many of these countries had become hostile towards the United States. They felt that in the past America had tried to dominate them. Roosevelt said he wanted all of these countries to be equal and independent.

In 1934 Roosevelt put the Good Neighbor policy into practice by withdrawing US troops from Haiti. The following year trade agreements were signed with Brazil, Colombia, Haiti and Honduras. Relations between the USA and Latin America were further improved with the conferences of Montevideo (1933), Buenos Aires (1936) and Lima (1938). In 1936 Roosevelt described the Good Neighbor policy in these words:

Peace, like charity, begins at home; and that's why we have begun at home, here in North and South and Central America ... to banish wars for ever from this vast portion of the earth.

The Open Door: trouble in China

At the turn of the century the United States' industrial output reached new heights. This led one politician to declare: 'American

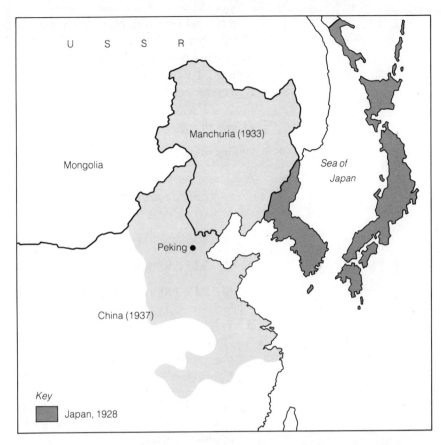

Japanese expansion in the Far East, 1933–7

U S S R

Mongolia

Manchuria (1933)

Sea of Japan

Peking •

China (1937)

Key

Japan, 1928

factories are producing more than the American people can use....
Fate has written our policy for us: the trade of the world shall be
ours.' In 1899 American economist Brooks Adams indicated where
new markets for American goods might be found: 'Our geographical
position, our wealth, our energy, permit us to enter the development
of eastern Asia and reduce it to part of our economic sphere.'

One country in particular attracted the greedy attention of
American industrialists. It was a country torn apart by the feuding of
rival warlords; a country where 400 million peasants lived per-
manently on the brink of starvation. Yet it was also an area with
enormous potential. Huge resources of coal and iron were still un-
tapped. Above all, its vast population meant that it could one day
provide a huge market for American products. That country was
China.

To make sure that trade with China could continue to grow,
America's politicians developed a policy known as the 'Open Door'.
The most important feature of the 'Open Door' was that China
should remain independent. America committed itself to keeping the
'door' to China open at all times. This placed it on a collision course
with a powerful adversary – Japan.

As the twentieth century progressed it became clear that Japan was
becoming increasingly ambitious. Its rulers decided that Japan's

commercial future depended on the acquisition of petroleum, bauxite and rubber in the Philippines, Burma and Malaya. This empire, led by Japan, was to be known as the Greater East Asia Co-prosperity Sphere. To complete that empire, Japan intended to conquer China. Its rulers were also prepared to go to war with the United States.

Using the evidence: the Open Door

Points to consider:

A *The Open Door*
   In 1899 US politician John Hay put forward the idea of an Open Door in China to free trade and investment.

   In 1908 Japan agreed to the idea of an Open Door.

   In 1922 Japan signed the Nine Power Treaty.

   In 1931 Japan sent troops into Manchuria.

B *Trade*
   China ... 'is the prize for which all energetic nations are grasping'. This statement comes from a book called *America's Economic Supremacy*, written in 1899.

   America's trade with China was slowing down in the 1930s, but trade with Japan was increasing. China was a backward, peasant society.

   US investments in China in 1931 = $200 million.
   US investments in Japan in 1935 = $466 million.

C *Armed forces*
   Japan probably has the most complete, well balanced, co-ordinated and therefore powerful fighting machine in the World today.

   US Ambassador in Tokyo, Joseph Grew, May 1933

   Our Navy was and probably still is actually inferior to the Japanese.

   F.D.R., August 1933

   Japan increased spending on its navy by 25 per cent in 1933.

D *Public opinion at home*
   Public opinion in America was very strongly against being involved in any war.

   Japanese historians call 1931–41 'the dark valley', because it was a time when personal freedom was under attack. Japan was being increasingly dominated by generals who were prepared to go to war to win land and glory.

E *Roosevelt's attitude*

A modern historian's view: 'He shared his fellow countrymen's sympathies for China and mistrusted the Japanese.'

Roosevelt's grandfather had made a fortune by trading with China.

The year is 1933. President Roosevelt is trying to decide which policy to follow in China. You have been asked to advise him. There are three main options:

a)   Take America's soldiers (approx. 2 500) out of China. Remove America's small fleet from the area. Allow the Open Door to be closed by the Japanese.

b)   Keep the number of troops and ships the same. Try to maintain the Open Door through good diplomacy with Japan.

c)   Build up US troops in China. Spend more money on the fleet in the Far East. Use force to stop the Japanese moving any further into China.

1   Using the information given under the heading 'Points to consider', list the advantages and disadvantages of each option.

2   Now place the options in order of preference, starting with the option that you think is best for the United States.

In January 1933 Roosevelt made it clear that he intended to stand by the Open Door policy. However, the weakness of America's Pacific Fleet and the small number of American troops in China, meant that he could not use force to defend China against Japan. On 7 March 1933 Roosevelt warned his Cabinet to 'avoid war with Japan'.

Meanwhile, power in Japan was passing into the hands of right-wing generals determined to see their country rise to a position of dominance in the Far East. In 1931 Japanese troops occupied the whole of Manchuria, in north-east China, and by the end of 1933 it was completely under their control. Sporadic fighting between China and Japan escalated to total war in 1937.

The road to war in the East, 1937–41

On the sultry night of July 1, 1937, the 'incident' that sparked off an all-out war [between China and Japan] occurred near Peking's historic Marco Polo Bridge. A jittery unit of the Kwantung Army, which had been sent in to guard Japanese interests in the city, opened fire on a nearby Nationalist troop encampment after one of its soldiers suddenly vanished into the dark. It turned out that he was merely relieving himself, but shots rang out and in three weeks what had started as another one of hundreds of 'incidents' was escalated into a pitched battle between the rival armies south of the old ... capital.

John Costello: *The Pacific War*, 1985

Roosevelt was alarmed by these events, especially as there was no sign that either side would back down. At least America was not directly involved – until, that is, the world's attention suddenly switched to a tiny US gunboat on the Yangtze River, deep inside China. On 12 December 1937 the *Panay* was sunk by the Japanese:

The Panay was churning 30 miles upstream when Lieutenant Commander James J. Hughes ... judged it safe to anchor his ship. Hands were piped to a leisurely Sunday lunch, which was interrupted at 1.30 pm when [Japanese] aircraft were sighted. 'They're letting go bombs, get under cover,' yelled Chief Quartermaster Land. Seconds after the captain reached the pilot house, it was ripped apart by an explosion. On deck, Universal Newsman Norman Alley instinctively grabbed his movie camera and kept it turning: he was amazed that the pilots, whose faces he could easily make out, persisted in their attack when they could clearly see the American flags.

... Two American seamen and one Italian journalist died. The survivors' ordeal was to continue for two more days as they struggled through to the Chinese lines, hunted by the Japanese.

John Costello: *The Pacific War*, 1985

USS Panay

Survivors from the USS Panay awaiting rescue having abandoned ship

---

Questions

1   How was it possible for fighting between Japan and China to affect America? To help you answer this question, refer back to the Open Door section.

2   The Japanese claimed that they had mistaken the USS *Panay* for a Chinese ship. How could the film shot by the newsman disprove this claim?

3   Roosevelt accepted Japan's explanation. He then censored the close-up shots in the film before it was shown to the American public. Can you explain why he did this?

America was outraged by the sinking of the *Panay* and war seemed inevitable. However, when the Japanese government accepted America's demand for a formal apology and full compensation, war was avoided. Roosevelt's problems with Japan were to flare up again, but for the time being events in Europe seemed even more alarming.

The road to war in Europe, 1935–9

I have said this before, but I shall say it again and again and again: your boys are not going to be sent into any foreign wars.
F.D.R., Boston, 1940

Despite the aggression of the Japanese in China and of Hitler in Europe, the pressure on Roosevelt to keep out of any war was immense. Many Americans could still vividly remember the horrors of World War I. Yet, in 1935, Roosevelt made a defence request for $1.1 billion, the largest peacetime defence budget in the history of the United States. Many Americans felt that they were going to be dragged once again into conflicts that seemed to have little to do with them. Senator Thomas Schall of Minnesota summed up how most people felt when he exclaimed: 'To hell with Europe and the rest of those nations!'

It was under these circumstances that Roosevelt accepted the terms of the Neutrality Act of 1935 which, like the later acts, was designed to keep America out of war by refusing to sell weapons or ammunition or to lend money to any country that was involved in a war. This applied equally to friendly countries, such as Britain, or hostile countries, such as Japan.

The ideas behind the Neutrality Acts made sense. By refusing to sell weapons to belligerents, America stood a much better chance of keeping out of any possible conflict in Europe. However, the increasingly aggressive actions of Germany and Japan made the Neutrality Acts seem more and more irrelevant. In March 1936 German soldiers reoccupied the Rhineland. Two years later Germany invaded Austria. In March 1939 Czechoslovakia was overrun. Then, in September 1939, Hitler sent his troops into Poland. America looked on as Great Britain and France declared war on Germany and Europe was plunged into conflict.

The end of neutrality

When Britain declared war on Germany in September 1939, the United States had to abide by its Neutrality legislation. The USA refused to sell arms, ammunition or implements of war to either side because, as Roosevelt put it, 'Our acts must be guided by one single thought – keeping America out of war.'

However, as the war progressed with a succession of German victories, Roosevelt became increasingly concerned that Britain would lose the war.

The measures described below were taken by Roosevelt to help Britain win the war, without directly involving America. He also took action to try to weaken the Japanese and to prevent them attacking American forces in the Far East.

November 1939	Roosevelt persuaded Congress to allow him to sell arms to belligerents, provided they paid cash and used their own ships for transport. He knew that Britain's navy was powerful enough to take advantage of this situation.
December 1940	*Lend-lease* In 1940 Churchill informed Roosevelt that Britain could overcome Hitler only if America provided ships, munitions and money. F.D.R. announced that America would provide war materials for Britain on the understanding that repayments would be made 'in kind' when the war was over.

1 August 1941	America refused to sell any oil to Japan. This left Japan with less than two years' supply. To obtain essential supplies, Japan would have to seize them.
August 1941	*The Atlantic Charter* A top-secret meeting between Roosevelt and Churchill took place on board the USS *Augusta*. Churchill told Roosevelt that Britain needed far more from America than money or guns. Roosevelt now realised that America had to join in the war. He was now prepared to lie to get the American public on his side.

USS Greer

On 4 September 1941 an American destroyer, USS *Greer*, was taking passengers and mail to Iceland when a British patrol aircraft informed the captain by radio that a German submarine was nearby. The USS *Greer* followed the submarine and passed on its exact location to the aircraft. The plane dropped some depth charges and then departed. The submarine fired two torpedoes at the *Greer* in retaliation but they missed.

The next day Roosevelt announced that the American destroyer had been deliberately attacked without warning. He declared that the time for action had come.

We have sought no shooting war even with Hitler. We do not seek it now. . . . But when you see a rattlesnake poised to strike, you do not wait until he has struck before you crush him. These Nazi submarines and raiders are the rattlesnakes of the Atlantic.

F.D.R., Address to the Nation, 11 September 1941

Questions

1 What words did F.D.R. use in his speech to persuade the American public that the Germans were untrustworthy?

2 Does F.D.R.'s conduct in the USS *Greer* incident change your view of his character?

One month after Roosevelt had announced a total ban on oil exports to Japan, Japan's ministers met to discuss war. Realising that 'it was almost impossible to expect a surrender from the United States', they decided to attempt a lightning takeover of South-East Asia and then to try to negotiate favourable terms with the USA.

The attack on Pearl Harbor

On Sunday 7 December 1941, at approximately 7.50 a.m. Hawaii time (1.20 p.m. Washington time), 190 Japanese dive bombers, torpedo planes and fighters attacked the American fleet and military installations at Pearl Harbor in Hawaii. The Americans were taken completely by surprise. In the attack, 2 403 of their men were killed and a further 1 178 were wounded. Seven battleships, along with most of the aircraft belonging to the army and navy, were destroyed or put out of action.

Below: *USS* West Virginia *and USS* Tennessee *after attack, 7 December 1941*

Inset: *the* Los Angeles Times' *report of the attack on Pearl Harbor*

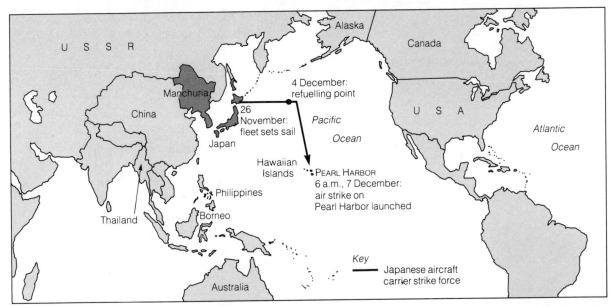

The raid on Pearl Harbor

Nowhere can the attack have been more terrifying than on the American battleship, *Oklahoma*. Devastated by four massive explosions and with water flooding through the below-deck hatches (which were still clipped open), the ship began to roll over. Many of the crew managed to scramble to safety moments before the ship turned upside down, but more than 400 sailors were trapped in the terrifying darkness of a flooding tomb.

'Rescue workers and divers spent two days trying to free the men, some of whom could be heard tapping desperately against the upturned hull of the *Oklahoma*. Only 30 of the trapped sailors were brought out alive.

How was it possible for the Americans to be taken so completely by surprise? Many historians think that they had a good idea that an attack was due, but that they did not know where it would take place. American intelligence experts believed at the time that Siam or Malaya or the Philippines were all more likely targets than Pearl Harbor. Some American historians have gone much further than this, claiming that Roosevelt deliberately encouraged the Japanese to attack an unguarded American fleet. Such an attack, they argue, finally provided the President with the public support he needed to declare war on Japan. The public, outraged by the apparent treachery of the Japanese, would finally be prepared to back the President and support a declaration of war.

Using the evidence: Pearl Harbor

Section 1: The President

a) (i) *We are likely to be attacked next Monday, for the Japs are notorious for attacking without warning. . . .*

F.D.R. to the Cabinet, 24 November 1941

49

(ii) *We must all prepare for real trouble possibly soon.*
A cable from F.D.R. to Churchill, 24 November 1941

b) *Roosevelt expressed concern about how to manoeuvre Japan into firing the first shot.*
Minutes of the meeting of F.D.R.'s War Council,
25 November 1941

c) *Dawn was already breaking over London on Sunday, December 7, when the clock struck midnight in the White House and the President retired for the night. Ready on his desk was a thirty-page draft of a speech to be delivered to Congress with which he hoped to win its support for declaring war if the Japanese attacked British or Dutch possessions in the Far East.*
John Costello: *The Pacific War*, 1985

Section 2: The President's advisers

a) *I lunched with the President today at his desk in the Oval Room. We were talking about things far removed from war when at about 1.40 Secretary Knox (of the navy) called and said that they had picked up a radio call from Honolulu ... advising ... that an air raid attack was on and that it was 'no drill'.*

I expressed the belief that there must be some mistake. . . . The President thought the report was probably true and thought it was just the kind of unexpected thing the Japanese would do.
Harry Hopkins' diary, 7 December 1941.
(Hopkins was one of Roosevelt's close friends and advisers)

b) *The President was deeply shaken ... graver than I had ever seen him.*
Attorney General Francis Biddle recalling the Cabinet meeting at the White House, 8.30 p.m., 7 December 1941

c) Frances Perkins was at the same Cabinet meeting as Francis Biddle (source b). She was troubled all evening by the expression on the President's face.

Sometimes I've seen it on his face when he was carrying through a plan which not everybody in the room approved and about which he didn't intend to tell too much. I've seen it on his face at times when I thought he was not making everything quite clear. . . .
Frances Perkins: *The Roosevelt I Knew*, 1946.
(Frances Perkins was a member of the Cabinet and one of Roosevelt's trusted friends)

50

Section 3: Warnings! Intelligence reports

a) *This dispatch is to be considered a war warning. . . .*
Aggressive action expected by Japan in the next few days.
[The target is expected to be] Philippines, Thai Peninsula or
Borneo.

> Warning to Pacific Fleet Commander in Chief,
> 27 November 1941

b) *On Sunday December 7 Japan's Ambassador in Washington*
phoned the Secretary of State to request an appointment at
precisely 1 o'clock, adding 'It is a matter of extreme
urgency'.
  Alarmed by this, the Army's Chief of Staff, General
Marshall, drafted a warning to be sent to Panama, the
Philippines, San Francisco and Hawaii. 'JUST WHAT
SIGNIFICANCE THE HOUR SET MAY HAVE WE DO NOT
KNOW BUT BE ON THE ALERT ACCORDINGLY.'
  Fatally, General Marshall sent the message by post rather
than by radio and it arrived too late.

> John Costello: *The Pacific War*, 1985

1   The evidence in section 1 suggests that Roosevelt expected a
    Japanese attack. In sections 2 and 3, how is this view (a)
    supported, and (b) contradicted?

2   Look again at sources b and c in section 2. You may be
    surprised to see that they both describe the same meeting.
    a) How do you explain the difference in the two accounts?
    b) Does this mean that one of these two pieces of evidence is
        inaccurate?
    c) Use the remaining evidence in all three sections to decide
        which source is most reliable, giving your reasons.

*F.D.R. signs a declaration of
war against Japan,
8 December 1941*

America at war!

Events now moved very quickly. On 8 December the President,
wearing a black armband of mourning, made an electrifying speech
to a packed Congress:

Yesterday, December 7, 1941 – a date which will live in infamy –
the United States was deliberately attacked by the naval and air
forces of the Empire of Japan. [Japan's] unprovoked and dastardly
attack [left no doubt] that our people, our territory and our interests
are in grave danger.

The President said that he was left with no alternative but to ask
Congress to declare war on Japan.

American propaganda poster
urges revenge for the
Japanese attack

With only one member of the Congress voting against the declaration of war, Roosevelt now knew that Japan's act of aggression had united the country behind him.

Three days later, on 11 December 1941, America's involvement in World War II became total. Hitler, describing Roosevelt as 'the man who is the main culprit in this war', announced that Germany was at war with the USA. Roosevelt summed up the situation when he told the British Prime Minister, Winston Churchill, 'We are all in the same boat now.'

ROOSEVELT-
AN ASSESSMENT

The death of the President

By April 1945 the end of World War II was in sight. America's involvement after the Japanese attack on Pearl Harbor had been the decisive factor in bringing about the defeat of Germany and Japan. However, the strain of leading America through the great Depression and then through the war had taken its toll on the President. It was decided that he should take a much needed holiday in Warm Springs, Georgia. A few days later, Roosevelt was dead:

Roosevelt's death is reported in The New York Times

Warm Springs on Thursday, April 12, was sunny and pleasant. Roosevelt sat in his cottage looking over his stamps. He had put on a

The New York Times.

| "All the News That's Fit to Print" | | LATE CITY EDITION Clearing and warm today. Fair, continued warm tomorrow. Temperature Yesterday—Max., 74; Min., 54 Sunrise today, 6:11; Sunset, 6:34 |

Copyright, 1945, by The New York Times Company.

VOL. XCIV...No. 31,856.   NEW YORK, FRIDAY, APRIL 13, 1945.   THREE CENTS

PRESIDENT ROOSEVELT IS DEAD;
TRUMAN TO CONTINUE POLICIES;
9TH CROSSES ELBE, NEARS BERLIN

U. S. AND RED ARMIES DRIVE TO MEET

Americans Across the Elbe in Strength
Race Toward Russians Who Have
Opened Offensive From Oder

WEIMAR TAKEN, RUHR POCKET SLASHED

Third Army Reported 19 Miles From Czechoslovak Border — British Drive Deeper in the North, Seizing Celle—Canadians Freeing Holland

By DREW MIDDLETON

PARIS, April 12—Thousands of tanks and a half million doughboys of the United States First, Third and Ninth Armies are racing through the heart of the Reich on a front of 150 miles, threatening Berlin, Leipzig and the last citadels of the Nazi power.

The Second Armored Division of the Ninth Army has crossed the Elbe River in force and is striking eastward toward Berlin, whose outskirts lie less than sixty miles to the east, according to reports from the front. [A report quoted by The United Press placed the Americans less than fifty miles from the capital.] Beyond Berlin the First White Russian Army has crossed the Oder on a wide front and a junction between the western and eastern Allies is not far off.

[The Moscow radio reported that heavy battles were raging west of the Oder before Berlin, indicating that Marshal Gregory K. Zhukoff had launched his drive toward the Reich's capital. The Soviet communiqué announced further progress by the Red Army forces in and around Vienna.]

Paris is wild with excitement tonight. A special edition of the newspaper France-Soir carries a report by the radio station "Voice of America" that places American forces fifteen and five-eighths miles from Berlin after an airborne landing that had linked up with Lieut. Gen. William H. Simpson's forces advancing eastward from the Elbe. This would put American forces only seventy-five

OUR OKINAWA GUNS DOWN 118 PLANES

Japanese Fliers Start 'Suicide' Attacks on Fleet, Sink a Destroyer, Hit Other Ships

By W. H. LAWRENCE

GUAM, Friday, April 13—Japan, attempting to halt the American march to Tokyo, has started 'desperate, suicidal' aerial attacks upon our ships and men in the Okinawa area, costing 118 planes on Thursday alone, Fleet Admiral

Franklin Delano Roosevelt
1882-1945

END COMES SUDDENLY AT WARM SPRINGS

Even His Family Unaware of Condition
as Cerebral Stroke Brings Death
to Nation's Leader at 63

ALL CABINET MEMBERS TO KEEP POSTS

Funeral to Be at White House Tomorrow,
With Burial at Hyde Park Home—
Impact of News Tremendous

By ARTHUR KROCK

WASHINGTON, April 12—Franklin Delano Roosevelt, War President of the United States and the only Chief Executive in history who was chosen for more than two terms, died suddenly and unexpectedly at 4:35 P. M. today at Warm Springs, Ga., and the White House announced his death at 5:48 o'clock. He was 63.

The President, stricken by a cerebral hemorrhage, passed from unconsciousness to death on the eighty-third day of his fourth term and in an hour of high triumph. The armies and fleets under his direction as Commander in Chief were at the gates of Berlin and the shores of Japan's home islands as Mr. Roosevelt died, and the cause he represented and led was nearing the conclusive phase of success.

Less than two hours after the official announcement, Harry S. Truman of Missouri, the Vice President, took the oath as the thirty-second President. The oath was administered by the Chief Justice of the United States, Harlan F. Stone, in a one-minute ceremony at the White House. Mr. Truman immediately let it be known that Mr. Roosevelt's Cabinet is remaining in office at his request, and that he had authorized Secretary of State Edward R. Stettinius Jr. to proceed with plans for the United Nations Conference on international organization at San Francisco, scheduled to begin April 25. A report was circulated that he leans somewhat to the idea

TRUMAN IS SWORN IN THE WHITE HOUSE

Members of Cabinet on Hand
as Chief Justice Stone
Administers the Oath

By C. P. TRUSSELL

WASHINGTON, April 12—Vice President Harry S. Truman of Missouri, standing erect, with his sharp features taut and looking straight ahead through his large, round glasses, became the thirty-second President of the United

53

dark blue suit and a Harvard-red tie for a painter who was doing his portrait. . . .

Suddenly the President groaned. He pressed and rubbed his temple hard – then the great head fell back inert. [Roosevelt had suffered a brain haemorrhage.] Carried to his bed, he lived, breathing heavily but unconscious, for about four hours. He died at 4.35 p.m.

James MacGregor Burns: *Roosevelt, the Lion and the Fox*, 1956

Roosevelt had been president for 12 years and had won four successive presidential elections. It is now time to assess his career.

Using the evidence: an assessment

A *He was the first fully modern president. He used the great crises which swept him into office to accustom the American people to look first to the White House for the solution of their political problems. The torrential activity of his first term greatly assisted this aim. . . . He was always news, always on the front pages of the newspapers. . . . In his 'fireside chats' on the radio he projected himself and his message into millions of homes. . . . He made extensive tours through America, so that hundreds of thousands saw for themselves the big smile.*

Hugh Brogan: *Purnell's History of the Twentieth Century*, 1968

B *From his first hours in office, Roosevelt gave people the feeling that they could confide in him directly. As late as the presidency of Herbert Hoover, one man, Ira Smith, had sufficed to take care of all the mail the White House received. Under Roosevelt, Smith had to acquire a staff of fifty people to handle the thousands of letters written to the president each week.*

William Leuchtenburg: *F.D.R. and the New Deal*, 1963

C *The figure of Roosevelt exhibited before the eyes of our people is a fiction. There was no such being as that noble, selfless, wise and farseeing combination of philosopher . . . and warrior which has been fabricated out of pure propaganda.*

John T. Flynn: *The Roosevelt Myth*, 1956

D *How did the New Deal come into existence? It was because there was an awfully sick patient called the United States of America, and it was suffering from a grave internal disorder – awfully sick – all kinds of things had happened to this patient. . . . And they sent for the doctor. And it was a long, long process — took several years before those ills . . . were remedied. . . .*

Franklin D. Roosevelt, December 1943

E   Some of Roosevelt's critics saw him as the enemy of the rich, taking their money away to spend on the poor.

Roosevelt the friend of the poor

Roosevelt the enemy of the rich

1   What criticisms of Roosevelt are provided in these sources?

2   What methods did Roosevelt use to maintain his own popularity with the American people?

3   Now provide your own assessment of the New Deal. Was it a success or a failure?

INDEX

WILBERFORCE
S.F.C.
LIBRARY